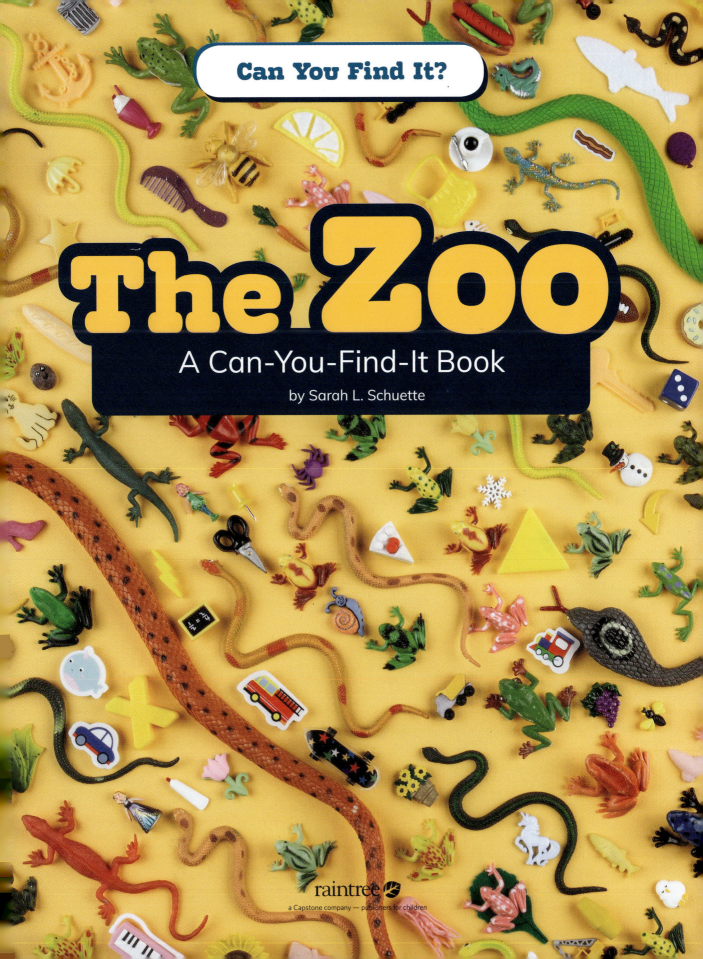

Zoo party

Can you find these things?

 whale

 eggs

 mouse

 glasses

 wizard

 ladybird

 blender

 snowman

 chick

 helmet

Penguin pool

Can you find these things?

motorbike

pepper

ant

chicken

 tractor tomato elephant lips aeroplane sunglasses

Stripes and spots

Can you find these things?

 moose

 drinks can

 jack

 boat

iron | fish tank | ice cube | tissue box | hammer | rubber duck

Flying monkeys

Can you find these things?

 avocado

 pin

 pencil

 dragon

mushroom

spider

fork

helicopter

rugby ball

teddy bear

Something fishy

Can you find these things?

 orange

 chainsaw

 deer

 pliers

 pear pig bus fox fortune cookie buoy

Big cat kingdom

Can you find these things?

 tractor

 dinosaur

 clothes peg

 hamster

 fish

 dolphin

 canoe

 hat

 wagon

 French fries

Panda garden

Can you find these things?

 pocket watch

 birdcage

 toilet paper

 alligator

 cookie

 ice lolly

 gingerbread man

 frog

 ice-cream cone

 sandwich

Feathered friends

Can you find these things?

 lamp

 worm

 skates

 crown

 rabbit

 tree

 turtle

 sword

 tennis racquet

 snail

Alphabet sea

Can you find these things?

 zip

 jet ski

 rake

 bread with jam

 butterfly

 violin

 comb

 stapler

 nose

 bucket

E for elephant

Can you find these things?

 walrus

 hard hat

 spoon

 camel

 lantern

 rubber

 marble

 cactus

 horseshoe

 cone

Slither and hop

Can you find these things?

 strawberry

 owl

 key

 umbrella

 scissors

 sheep

 skateboard

 light bulb

 toothpaste

 mitten

Lunch munch

Can you find these things?

 ox

 plate of cookies

 dragon

 toaster

 taco   tent   hedgehog   clipboard   boot   cat

Butterfly beauty

Can you find these things?

 rhinoceros

 screw

 aubergine

 party bag

 knife

 goldfish cracker

 teapot

 paintbrush

 log cabin

 Earth

Challenge puzzle
A zoo for you!
Can you find these things?

 sloth

 sweetcorn

 pickle

 watermelon

Turn the page for the answer key!

globe	pretzel	pirate ship	hand	bell	hot dog

Challenge puzzle: A zoo for you! answer key

Psst! Did you know that Pebs the Pebble was hiding in EVERY PUZZLE in this book?

It's true! Go back and look!

Look for all the other books in this series:

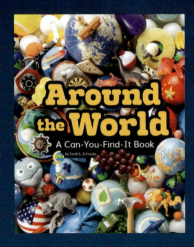
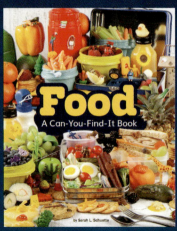
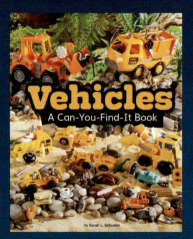

Raintree is an imprint of Capstone Global Library Limited, a company incorporated in England and Wales having its registered office at 264 Banbury Road, Oxford, OX2 7DY – Registered company number: 6695582

www.raintree.co.uk
myorders@raintree.co.uk

Text and illustrations © Capstone Global Library Limited 2021
The moral rights of the proprietor have been asserted.

All rights reserved. No part of this publication may be reproduced in any form or by any means (including photocopying or storing it in any medium by electronic means and whether or not transiently or incidentally to some other use of this publication) without the written permission of the copyright owner, except in accordance with the provisions of the Copyright, Designs and Patents Act 1988 or under the terms of a licence issued by the Copyright Licensing Agency, Barnard's Inn, 86 Fetter Lane, London, EC4A 1EN (www.cla.co.uk). Applications for the copyright owner's written permission should be addressed to the publisher.

Jill Kalz, editor; Heidi Thompson, designer; Marcy Morin, set stylist;
Morgan Walters, media researcher; Kathy McColley, production specialist

ISBN 978 1 4747 9572 2 (hardback)
ISBN 978 1 4747 9608 8 (paperback)

British Library Cataloguing in Publication Data
A full catalogue record for this book is available from the British Library.

All photos by Capstone Studio: Karon Dubke

Printed and bound in India.